JN440339

I'll Write Again Tomorrow

# I'll Write Again Tomorrow

A collection of new poems by Song Kyeong-dong
Translated by Brother Anthony of Taizé

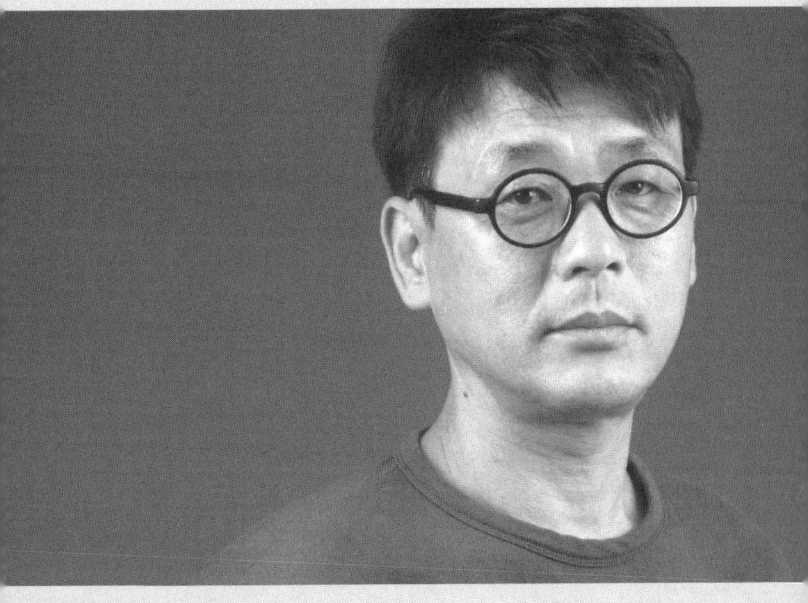

아시아

# Contents

# I'LL WRITE AGAIN TOMORROW

## Diary

The shy diary I wrote as a child
is still well hidden in the closet.

The diary written once I was an adult
is all inscribed in police reports and prosecutor's indictments
and is carefully stored in the government archives.

A diary written with you,
with your you,
since it can't be written well alone.

## Pride

When I was working for the Blacklist Truth Commission.
I arduously compiled a list of 249 cultural and artistic figures
that the National Intelligence Service
had illegally inspected in the past.

The names were labeled A, B, and C.
Luckily, my name was among the twenty-two A's.
If it had been a B or a C
I wouldn't have been able to believe in the raison d'être
of the National Intelligence Service.

# The Center of the World

In September 2003, I traveled
to Cancun, Mexico to protest.
The anti-globalization fighters
who came from all over the world
to block the WTO World Summit were splendid
and I also remember the martyr Lee Kyung-hae stabbing himself in the chest
on a barbed-wire fence and falling like a dead leaf.

But really what I can't forget after all this time
in the world's best vacation spot with its emerald shore,

in the construction site of a new building in the city center
was a barefoot boy laborer
with a huge hammer and chisel
drying up like a blackened pollack in the scorching sun.

A decade or more later,
as a poet invited
to a book fair,
I visited various places in the United States,
called the center of world capital,
but again there's just one scene I remember.

In downtown Chicago at dusk, in a small gap between buildings,
a black man about my age,
wrapped in a filthy blanket,
holding two small children in his arms.
With a gaze as wistful as a pale crescent moon on a dark night,
their sad eyes looked up at me as I stood there.

What I can't forget is misery, not glory,
The center of the world is the place where my heart was broken
rather than the place where I made up my mind

A place where someone's tears and wounds are, that's where the world's best forces emerge.

## A is B

The Myanmar poet Khet Thi,
who said he would be neither a hero nor a coward,
was found murdered on the street on May 8, 2021,
one day after being arrested by the coup d'état's military.

The junta had ripped the heart from his body
and abandoned it.
He had written, "They shoot in the head,
but they don't know the revolution is in the heart."

It's surprisingly simple to teach evil spirits
who don't know the deep meaning of metaphors
that A is B.
Now I'm telling them I'm Khet Thi.

# The Old House

They said the old house had to be saved first
so lit a fire to keep it warm.

They laid firewood in the warm fireplaces of corporations and banks
and lit the fire.

As soon as floor grew a little bit warm
austerity theories emerged about having to save firewood.

Even after many people moved away from the thin ice of returning austerity
and the discriminatory chill winds of the state,

The old house's broken heating system

was never fixed.

## A Maze of History

Of the nine justices of the United States Supreme Court,
when asked how many women would be enough,
Ruth Ginsburg said, "Nine."
Until Ginsburg's confirmation in 1993
all nine Supreme Court justices were men
and no one questioned that.

Of course, we know that Ginsburg, who had worked for the extension of women's rights,
agreed that non-Christian lands could be colonized under the Doctrine of Discovery,
denying Native Americans the right to self-

determination,
sided with the multinational corporation Dole,
condoning environmental destruction and corporate monopolies.
When the American Football player Colin Kaepernick refused the Pledge of Allegiance
and the National Anthem in protest over black people shot and killed by white police officers,
Ginsburg followed in Trump's footsteps, who called him a "son of a bitch,"
calling Kaepernick's actions "dumb and disrespectful."

It's just that the world is complicated,

something we must never forget.

In April 2022, Ketanji Jackson became the first black woman to be appointed to the U.S. Supreme Court.

What questions will she face and what kind of historical maze will she walk? How transparent and honest can she be regarding everything that is not the United States?

## Tearful Spring

Plod. Plod.

A crippled man with one leg shorter than the other
is walking up the Doksan-dong Pass,
his left foot and right foot working like pistons.

Carrying a pair of rusty iron gates, bigger than his handcart,
his crooked mouth curls like a flower petal,
he's so excited.

All holy things
are poor.

## Observing Officials

Your mouths
are like giant sewers.

The halls you frequent
are like septic tanks.

Every time you open your mouths a stinking
flood
of lies, corruption, and lust emerges.

Highly pigmented and greasy,
it doesn't break down easily.

This vast ocean is always much troubled.

## Eight Deadly Sins

In the Mahatma Gandhi Memorial Park in
Delhi, India,
inscribed on stones
there are seven vices
that during his lifetime he deemed to be sins.

Politics without philosophy.
Economics without morals.
Wealth without labor.
Education without character.
Science without humanity.
Pleasure without ethics.
Religion without devotion.

How good if only a world came about
from which the wicked who thrive on these seven things
were excommunicated.
The one thing he left out
was 'citizens who don't fight.'

## A World Out of Touch

I feel like I'm on Mars.
After tens of thousands of lightning strikes in California,
wildfires have been burning for a month now,
burning an area more than twenty times the size of Seoul.
And it's all because of climate change.

In the Brazilian Amazon jungle, the lungs of the planet,
producing 20 percent of the world's oxygen,
100,000 wildfires have been burning for a year.
This is also due to climate change.

In February 2020, summer arrived at Marambio Station in Antarctica,
38 degrees were recorded in Verkhoyansk, in the Arctic,
while the Greenland ice cap, the canary in the coal mine of climate change,
is melting at a record rate of 532 trillion liters a year.
This is also due to climate change.

In the Andes and the Himalayan plateaus,
glacial lakes, mirrors of the Earth, reflecting the sun's heat
and cooling the earth's surface for hundreds of

millions of years,

have increased in size by 1.5 times in the last decade.

This is also due to climate change.

It's not even the rainy season on the Korean Peninsula.

Three typhoons in a row

The reason for the outbreaks of SARS, Swine Flu, MERS, Ebola ...

and COVID-19 is also the climate crisis.

Climate disaster is due to climate change.

That's too much.

They don't say that the destruction of the Amazon rainforest
is the result of Brazil's new dictator,
Bolsonaro, who is pushing for indiscriminate development
in the interest of multinational capital.

That's too much.
The don't say that climate crisis, climate disaster,
is due to the insatiable greed of global oil capital
caused by a market that encourages overproduction and endless consumption.

and the myth of development and progress.

Education, the media, culture, politics exaggerate
when they don't say that it's because of a
civilization of plunder and greed
for the sake of unlimited monopoly and
accumulation
by the world's 0.1% of capitalists,
for the astronomical comfort and affluence of
the first world.

The culprit of all this apocalypse and
destruction
is not wildfires, not heat waves, not particulate

matter, not the hole in the ozone layer.
It's not hurricanes and tornadoes and melting glaciers,
not bats, not pangolins, not wild boars, not cats,
not SARS, not MERS, not Ebola, not COVID-19.

It's humans themselves,
who have lost touch with themselves,
finally not coming to terms with our finite lives,
our eternal ignorance of an infinite world,
not becoming utterly simple.

Like dominoes falling,
the disasters of the world
will never cease,
catastrophes
will not stop.

## What Spring Is For

An acquaintance of mine who always cares for her surroundings
says Spring is here, so let's share pretty scarves.
She brings nine of them
and tells me about the different ways to use them.

You can wear them around your neck
or as a towel for wiping sweat.
For women, they can be used as knee covers in the summer
or as a head covering to keep off light rain.
or put one on the glass of a table
to decorate it.

But poor me, I can't stop thinking of them
as face coverings to prevent being recognized
by the police during rallies.
Depending on how you live,
the right springtime uses
are so different.

## I Lived Well Once

I do not regret
that my poems
lack the praise and admiration of green nature.

I do not lament
that my poems lack the lamentations and exultation
of tender love.

I do not worry
that my poems
lack worship and wonder at the vast universe.

I do not deplore

that my poems
do not reflect a radiant outlook and a steadfast optimism about history.

For example, the people who work in front of hot ovens,
who work in the blazing heat and cold,
amidst exploitation, discrimination, violence, and indignity.

because I once stood beside them,
I do not regret
that my poems are filled with their lowly, cramped stories.

Since I was once insulated
from a world that is sufficiently noble and happy
and could communicate with a world where pain is all there is.

I do not regret
that my poetry was not able to take even a few steps away
from those screams and cries.

## My Life's Study

My life's study that I yearn for
was a worker's meeting room, cramped with even just five people sitting,
where a dozen would gather,
read texts and discuss
and the factory wall where I went strolling
to see the roses that burst like blood through the wire fence in spring;
the city center alleyways where we ran to escape tear gas and riot police;
sometimes, it was a small seaside village behind the Pyeongtaek U.S. military base
where the original inhabitants of the reclaimed land struggled to survive,

it was inside the sweltering container
where fired irregular women workers had been fasting for 94 days,
the abandoned house we occupied under the watchtower
where five victims of evictions had burned to death.
It was the dawn sea that greeted us by dancing the liberation dance
beneath the high-altitude sit-in on Hanjin Heavy Industries No. 85 crane,
and it was in the tent in front of Daehan Gate in central Seoul
sheltering the altar with photos of twenty-two

faceless victims
 fired by Ssangyong Motor Co..
 It has been on top of countless CC camera towers, electricity transmission towers,
 the Han River bridge, advertising towers in the city center, factory chimneys
 that people climbed like sparrows to stage high-altitude sit-in protests.
 'Remember Sewolho,' 'People are more important than profits.'
 It was in front of the Blue House gates on June 10, 2014
 after hours of trying to get in amidst thunderstorms and hail.

‘Arrest Park Geun-hye;’ ‘Arrest Lee Jae-yong.’
It was in the unheated tent of a one-person demonstration
under the snow-covered statue of Yi Sun-sin in Gwanghwamun Plaza.

My study, where I used to read the world like that
was not some ivory-tower authority or lofty words.
It was certainly not an objective narrative.
It was not a belated critique or a metaphysics.

There were more tasks to embrace

than sentences to underline.
No room for subtext and metaphor.
Simply inscribing the fury of frankness.
Such is the study of my life.

# I'll Write Again Tomorrow

I'm going to stop writing
memorial poems.

I'm going to stop writing
about workers who were laid off

I'm going to stop writing
about abandoned human beings..

I'm going to stop writing
poems burning with hostility.

I'm going to stop writing
poems that in the end burn me up.

I'm going to stop writing.

Today's dawn has already arrived.

## Drowning in Debt

What beautiful words
The Apostle Paul said:
"Owe no one anything except the debt of love."

But if you think about it.
even in Paul's day, 2000 years ago.
there was a propertied class that lived indebted to someone.

Mother, with a back bent from a lifetime in the proletariat,
often recalled the days of her life.
Who ever wanted to be in debt to someone?

## I Just Want Us to Be Friends

I don't want you to change.

I don't want you to lower yourself.

I don't want to be the driver of our relationship.

I don't want me to be the helper.

I just want you to trust me as someone safe.

I just want to be your friend.

# The Duty of Hoping

Hope
comes with obligations.

To want something badly
necessarily includes a firm commitment
not to surrender to despair,
but to act.

When you dream of love,
all hope that does not accept the obligation to act
as if putting everything on the line
is pretense.

## The Lull

A protest demonstration that lasts as announced
from this time to that time
is just too creepy.

Because people have wrongly learned
that things must be rejected and resisted
from head to toe.

It's because people have wrongly learned
that no protest or rebellion was ever made
by sagely following the permitted path.

People who want everything to be resolved

quietly and amicably
call me an immature child.

## Trees. Trees.

There's a pretty name tag hanging on a tree
in the garden in front of a hotel.
It kindly informs us that the tree is a red pine
that blossoms in May and bears fruit the following year in September.

People
mostly already wilt in their twenties
and spend long years seemingly dead.

The name tag on the breast of the young part-time worker
pushing boxes of food waste out the back door of the hotel.

doesn't say when he might be allowed
to blossom.

## Blacklisted

After the candlelight vigils,
once the new government took over,
the phone would occasionally stutter then cut off.
I wondered who was censoring me again.
Was it the National Intelligence Service or the National Police Intelligence Division?
The National Security Support Company, renamed the Military Intelligence Service?
Or a private organization of chaebols trying to get the conservatives back in power?
At that, my consciousness sank.

This might be being recorded.

I had to choose words that wouldn't get me caught,
avoid naming specific people on the phone
and keep my emails as bland as possible.
We're poor, but sometimes
I have to replace my computer hard disk. This year
I wonder how many times my phone records have been checked
and every time I used a credit card
I wonder if it was evidence of anything.

This kind of thing i
is called self-censorship.

It drives people crazy.
It's how people conform to the status quo.
This is how freedom of speech, press, association, expression.
all autonomy and creativity
are destroyed.

And that's how people feed on the blood
of independent free spirits,
while even depressed thoughts that
the specters of totalitarianism will be reborn,
in retrospect,
were the culmination of a long process of inspection and censorship.

# POET'S NOTE

Depression is a great excuse for my poor health.

Grief is a very good cloak to hide my empty ignorance.

Resignation is a very good tool to bury my laziness.

Capital and power love our depression, sadness, resignation, and frustration. Fruits with high sugar content grow in clusters on top of thoroughly mixed manure.

... It seems like I had a good time until yesterday, with a lot to say.

But what good is that?

There are days when I can't think of anything to say and the world and life seem hazy and dim like a fog.

It's a little like that today.

I'll write again tomorrow.

# POET'S ESSAY

## A Poem measuring 2.2 Square Yards

...Sometimes I think of the solitary confinement cell in Busan Detention Centre, where I was briefly detained after the Hope Bus movement against the Hanjin Heavy Industries layoffs in 2011. It was a tiny space of only 2.2 square yards, with a small toilet attached to it, with a single peephole, and I was wary of whether I should be enjoying such happiness.

The six months of being on the run, wondering when I would be arrested, were over, and the struggle had been won, so I had nothing to regret. I felt like I could live on my own, away from the work days that never gave me a day's rest, away from the tensions and arguments over the direction of the movement, away from the hurt I was causing people through my own inadequacies. I was happy to wash my face and do the dishes in the toilet bowl, which was thick with yellow and black phosphorus like a scab, with two tubes of toothpaste.

Through the bars, I'd even photosynthesise, bathing in the sunlight that only visited me briefly in the morning, and I was grateful to be reminded that human fake mouths and shitty backsides aren't that far away, or at least that I'm one of them.

... In my not-so-distant memory, I also recall a small, one-person, one-touch tent that was set up under the statue of Yi Sun-sin in Gwanghwamun, Seoul, sometime in the winter of 2016 and spring of 2017, right in the middle of the history of removing yet another totalitarian wannabe dictator and her minions from power.

It was a toy-like tent that inflated into a circle in an instant if you threw it into the air. I didn't know if I could make it work, and even if I did, I didn't know when the police would tear it down, so I got the cheapest one I could find in the malls of Cheonggyecheon. It was less than a yard long, when I sat up, my head touched the ceiling, and when I lay down, my head and toes touched the top and bottom. All I had was a lantern, some toiletries, underwear and winter clothes. The bathroom at a nearby hotel had hot water, so I was able to wash my face occasionally that winter. At night, I slept with a few hand warmers in my sleeping bag, and I think the only real heater was my body, which was 36.5 degrees warm. When I woke up, the heat from my body and the cold outside had met on the ceiling of the tent and dripped down, soaking my sleeping bag.

But I was happy, grateful that I could be in the middle of this history, and I learnt that I could live simply without having to live in a tower palace, without having all the furniture and crockery and appliances.

... and I hope that the language of my poems will not forget those small lessons learned in the field. May my poetry not lean on plausible deniability, may it not mask or embellish the present me with the past me that has already passed. I hope the things I get angry about don't harden into conventions, and I hope the things I love are written down waiting to be deepened.

# COMMENTARY

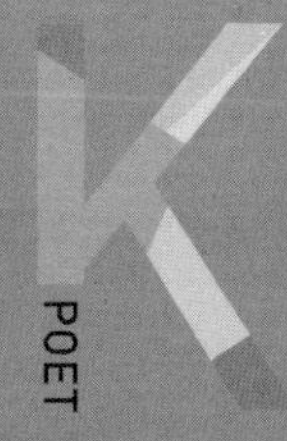

# The Center of the World with Its Tears and Wounds

Ko Myeong-cheol
(Literary Critic, Professor at Kwangwoon University)

## 1.

The poet Song Kyeong-dong speaks without hesitation. "For example, the people who work in front of hot ovens, / who work in the blazing heat and cold, / amidst exploitation, discrimination, violence, and indignity, // Because I once stood beside them, / I do not regret / that my poems are filled with their lowly, cramped stories." (From: "I Lived Well Once"), and "All holy things / are poor" (From:

"Tearful Spring"). In this way, he writes poetry beside people who are living the reality of a low, mean and insignificant life. So, the study where he ponders poetry is not a respectable writing space, but amidst the realities of a life full of the tyranny, exploitation, and death that are occurring everywhere in our era.

2.

My study, where I used to read the world like that
was not some ivory-tower authority or lofty words.
It was certainly not an objective narrative.
It was not a belated critique or a metaphysics.

There were more tasks to embrace

than sentences to underline.
No room for subtext and metaphor.
Simply inscribing the fury of frankness.
Such is the study of my life.
— ("My Life's Study")

The basis of Song Kyeong-dong's poetry, in other words, the reality of Song Kyeong-dong's poetics can be recognized at once. Just as his poetry spreads wide and deep roots in the field of life, the struggles of his life and poetry against the vicious world of evil and infinite do not make detours. "Straightforward anger" becomes a poetic sensitivity generated by the political and ethical sense of his poetry, which endorses the power of poetic practice to go beyond the boundaries of the poetic text and intervene directly in the realities of life. For example, inscribed on stones the seven vices that Gandhi regarded as sins: "Politics without philosophy. / Economics without morals. / Wealth without labor. / Education without character. / Science without humanity. / Pleasure without ethics. / Religion without devotion," but "How good if only a world came about / from which the wicked who thrive on these seven things / were excommunicated. / The one thing he left out / was 'citizens who don't fight.'" ("Eight Deadly Sins"). Thus Song Kyeong-dong draws attention to the political and ethical sense and practice that if we recognize Gandhi's seven sins clearly, we should not be satisfied with that, but should strive to eradicate them, we should never stop fighting fiercely against them. In other words, the knowledge of contradictions, injustices, and unclean things and the resistance and struggle against them should go hand in hand, and if they do not, Song modifies Gandhi's precepts into 'eight sins'. In this way, the poetic resistance and struggle against these "eight sins" is very relevant to understanding Song's poetics.

3.

In this regard, what is particularly noticeable in this collection of poems is the evil witnessed in the global capitalist system, the poet's critical resistance and struggle against it, and the poetic practice of international popular solidarity.

> But really what I can't forget after all this time
> in the world's best vacation spot with its emerald shore,

in the construction site of a new building in the city center
was a barefoot boy laborer
with a huge hammer and chisel
drying up like a blackened pollack in the scorching sun.

(.....)

In downtown Chicago at dusk, in a small gap between buildings,
a black man about my age,
wrapped in a filthy blanket,
holding two small children in his arms.
With a gaze as wistful as a pale crescent moon on a dark night,
their sad eyes looked up at me as I stood there.

What I can't forget is misery, rather than glory.
Maybe places where the heart grows dark and crumbles,
not places where goals are set, that are the center of the world.
Maybe the place where there are tears and wounds
is the noblest place in this world.
— (From: "The Center of the World")

The poet's memories of Cancun, Mexico, that he visited "to block the WTO World Summit," and New York, New York, where he was a "poet / invited to a book fair," are of "a barefoot boy laborer" doing construction work under harsh conditions and "a black man/ holding two small children in his arms" enduring a night of hardship in an inner-city slum, as "their sad eyes looked up at me." For the poet, these figures are not unfamiliar. The lives of the politically and economically disadvantaged, despite their different skin colors and concrete circumstances, are not getting any better under the tangible and intangible power of the various institutions that further consolidate the political and economic vested interests that support the capitalist world system. They are relegated to the back corners of the world as they are increasingly dominated by the powers at the center of the world. However, this is where the poet's resistance and struggle lead to the imagination of subversion. The very place where the underdog is relegated, "where there are tears and wounds," is not a place of exclusion, exile, and abandonment from the corrupted power of the center, but a place of hope where we can clearly look at and recognize the injustice and corruption of the center, and thus energize a life of renewal through resistance and struggle; in other words, practice the "uneasy revolution" that we have been losing. For him, the Mexican, American, and Korean people's solidarity is therefore a natural practice of international people's movements in the global capitalist system. This is also evident in the poem "A is B", in which he stands in solidarity with the noble will of a Myanmar poet (Khet Thi) who lost his life in the coup d'état during the country's pro-democracy movement.

4.

In this collection of poems, Song cultivates a

political and ethical sense of poetry, the kind of poetic practice that poetic sensitivity generates. As we can see clearly in "all hope that does not accept the obligation to act ... is pretense." ("The Duty of Hoping"), gazing at the world's evils then resisting, struggling against them, and overthrowing them is the essence of a realist who confronts our lives and reality unflinchingly. So, I dare say, it would be difficult to overlook the following apocalyptic warning from the realist Song Kyeong-dong.

> It's humans themselves,
> who have lost touch with themselves,
> finally not coming to terms with our finite lives,
> our eternal ignorance of an infinite world,
> not becoming utterly simple.

Like dominoes falling,
the disasters of the world
will never cease,
catastrophes
will not stop.
—(From: "A World Out of Touch")

# PRAISE FOR SONG KYEONG-DONG

He is consistently a poet of bias and partiality. He is either a misfit in a system that is unlikely to change throughout his life, or he is a Class A blacklist. A person whose heart is set on 'misery, not glory.' He thought it was Kim Nam-jo and went looking for her, but when he met Kim Nam-joo, his life was turned upside down. Thus, he is the person who created the unique genre of rage called Song Kyeong-dong. He tells us we have still not been able to leave 'Yongsan Tragedy Station' or 'Itaewon Tragedy Station'. He tells us we are living in the same world as the evil spirits who ripped out the poet's heart and threw it away. A lonely person standing guard and shouting. A person who shouts that the things that truly need to be ripped out are 'these dazzling ruins.' His deep plain speaking, like a friend playing ducks and drakes across a river, made me look around as, one after another, ripples, firm but smooth and stinging yet warm, came rushing in again.

Moon Dong-man (Poet)

Here is a poet who is arrested while testifying to the barbarism and violence of this world and dreaming of a subversive world. One who testifies to the fate of those living underground through poetry, a subversive tool. A descendant of poets who were once exiled. One with the code name of a butterfly dreaming of revolution or a temporary worker who wants to be a warrior more than a poet. One who sings for souls for whom red lights are turned on at every stop in life. A person who takes work clothes and tools out of a burning basement and turns them into living poetry. A poet who writes down the tears shed by other mirrors of workers: hands, wrinkles, ladders, tools, and work clothes. Song Kyung-dong, a poet who writes industrial-accident-poetry for the living and condolence poetry for the dead.

Lee Sul-ya (Poet)

When I read his poetry, I feel as if I am standing in front of French painter Georges-Henri Rouault's series "Miserere." Rouault once said, 'Do not run away from pain or misery. Do not give up the smallest fragment of what you feel so well within yourself for fleeting interests, privileges, and temporary fame.' In all of Song Kyeong-dong's poetry, this principle resonates deeply like an ethical imperative.

However, what is really surprising about this collection of poems is that the poet's voice, that stays close to pain, is so clear. I think I can find the reason for that clarity in the reflections of Primo Levi, the greatest master of pain and sorrow. Levi said that the voices of those who die alone in the misery of the world, those who reach despair, are unclear and ambiguous and resemble the cries of animals. However, he added, the voice of a person trying to convey pain beside an incomprehensible cry must be clear. It can be clear and useless, clear and dishonest, clear and shallow, but if it is not clear, there is no message. I want to add these words again and whisper them in Levi's ear: Here are poems that are clear, useful, honest, and noble.

Jin Eun-young (Poet)

K-POET
I'll Write Again Tomorrow

**Written by** Song Kyeong-dong
**Translated by** Brother Anthony of Taizé
**Published by** ASIA Publishers
**Address** 445, Hoedong-gil, Paju-si, Gyeonggi-do, Korea
(Seoul Office: 161-1, Seodal-ro, Dongjak-gu,Seoul, Korea)
**Email** bookasia@hanmail.net
**ISBN** 979-11-5662-317-5 (set) | 979-11-5662-655-8 (04810)
First published in Korea by ASIA Publishers 2023

This book is published with the support of the Literature Translation Institute of Korea (LTI Korea).

## K-픽션 시리즈 | Korean Fiction Series

〈K-픽션〉 시리즈는 한국문학의 젊은 상상력입니다. 최근 발표된 가장 우수하고 흥미로운 작품을 엄선하여 출간하는 〈K-픽션〉은 한국문학의 생생한 현장을 국내외 독자들과 실시간으로 공유하고자 기획되었습니다. 〈바이링궐 에디션 한국 대표 소설〉 시리즈를 통해 검증된 탁월한 번역진이 참여하여 원작의 재미와 품격을 최대한 살린 〈K-픽션〉 시리즈는 매 계절마다 새로운 작품을 선보입니다.

001 버핏과의 저녁 식사-**박민규** Dinner with Buffett-**Park Min-gyu**

002 아르판-**박형서** Arpan-**Park hyoung su**

003 애드벌룬-**손보미** Hot Air Balloon-**Son Bo-mi**

004 나의 클린트 이스트우드-**오한기** My Clint Eastwood-**Oh Han-ki**

005 이베리아의 전갈-**최민우** Dishonored-**Choi Min-woo**

006 양의 미래-**황정은** Kong's Garden-**Hwang Jung-eun**

007 대니-**윤이형** Danny-**Yun I-hyeong**

008 퇴근-**천명관** Homecoming-**Cheon Myeong-kwan**

009 옥화-**금희** Ok-hwa-**Geum Hee**

010 시차-**백수린** Time Difference-**Baik Sou linne**

011 올드 맨 리버-**이장욱** Old Man River-**Lee Jang-wook**

012 권순찬과 착한 사람들-**이기호** Kwon Sun-chan and Nice People-**Lee Ki-ho**

013 알바생 자르기-**장강명** Fired-**Chang Kang-myoung**

014 어디로 가고 싶으신가요-**김애란** Where Would You Like To Go?-**Kim Ae-ran**

015 세상에서 가장 비싼 소설-**김민정** The World's Most Expensive Novel-**Kim Min-jung**

016 체스의 모든 것-**김금희** Everything About Chess-**Kim Keum-hee**

017 할로윈-**정한아** Halloween-**Chung Han-ah**

018 그 여름-**최은영** The Summer-**Choi Eunyoung**

019 어느 피씨주의자의 종생기-**구병모** The Story of P.C.-**Gu Byeong-mo**

020 모르는 영역-**권여선** An Unknown Realm-**Kwon Yeo-sun**

021 4월의 눈-**손원평** April Snow-**Sohn Won-pyung**

022 서우-**강화길** Seo-u-**Kang Hwa-gil**

023 가출-**조남주** Run Away-**Cho Nam-joo**

024 연애의 감정학-**백영옥** How to Break Up Like a Winner-**Baek Young-ok**

025 창모-**우다영** Chang-mo-**Woo Da-young**

026 검은 방-**정지아** The Black Room-**Jeong Ji-a**

027 도쿄의 마야-**장류진** Maya in Tokyo-**Jang Ryu-jin**

028 홀리데이 홈-**편혜영** Holiday Home-**Pyun Hye-young**

029 해피 투게더-**서장원** Happy Together-**Seo Jang-won**

030 골드러시-**서수진** Gold Rush-**Seo Su-jin**

031 당신이 보고 싶어하는 세상-**장강명** The World You Want to See-**Chang Kang-myoung**

032 지난밤 내 꿈에-**정한아** Last Night, In My Dream-**Chung Han-ah**

Special 휴가중인 시체-**김중혁** Corpse on Vacation-**Kim Jung-hyuk**

Special 사파에서-**방현석** Love in Sa Pa-**Bang Hyeon-seok**